DAVID MA

Speed-the-Plow

METHUEN DRAMA

A Methuen Drama Modern Play

5 7 9 10 8 6

First published in Great Britain in 1988 by Methuen Drama

Methuen Drama
A & C Black Publishers Ltd
36 Soho Square
London W1D 3QY

Reissued with a new cover design in 1994

This edition, with new cover design, published
in 2002 by Methuen Publishing Limited

A CIP catalogue record for this book is available from the British Library

ISBN 978 0 413 19280 6

Printed and bound in Great Britain by
CPI Cox & Wyman, Reading, RG1 8EX

THIS PLAY IS DEDICATED
TO HOWARD ROSENSTONE

Which is the most reasonable, and does his duty best: he who stands aloof from the struggle of life, calmly contemplating it, or he who descends to the ground, and takes his part in the contest? "That philosopher," Pen said, "had held a great place amongst the leaders of the world, and enjoyed to the full what it had to give of rank and riches, renown and pleasure, who came, weary-hearted, out of it, and said that all was vanity and vexation of spirit. Many a teacher of those whom we reverence, and who steps out of his carriage up to his carved cathedral place, shakes his lawn ruffles over the velvet cushion, and cries out that the whole struggle is an accursed one, and the works of the world are evil. Many a conscience-stricken mystic flies from it altogether, and shuts himself out from it within convent walls (real or spiritual), whence he can only look up to the sky, and contemplate the heaven out of which there is no rest, and no good.

"But the earth, where our feet are, is the work of the same Power as the immeasurable blue yonder, in which the future lies into which we would peer. Who ordered sickness, ordered poverty, failure, success—to this man a foremost place, to the other a nameless struggle with the crowd—to that a shameful fall, or paralyzed limb or sudden accident—to each some work upon the ground he stands on, until he is laid beneath it."

THACKERAY,
Pendennis

Speed-the-Plow was first presented in a New York Broadway production by Lincoln Center Theater at the Royale Theater, opening on May 3, 1988, with the following cast:

BOBBY GOULD	Joe Mantegna
CHARLIE FOX	Ron Silver
KAREN	Madonna

Directed by Gregory Mosher
Designed by Michael Merritt
Costumes by Nan Cibula
Lighting by Kevin Rigdon

This production subsequently transferred to the National Theatre on January 25, 1989, with the following changes:

BOBBY GOULD	Colin Stinton
CHARLIE FOX	Alfred Molina
KAREN	Rebecca Pidgeon

SPEED-THE-PLOW

CHARACTERS

BOBBY GOULD, CHARLIE FOX, two men around forty
KAREN, a woman in her twenties

SCENES

ONE: Gould's office, morning
TWO: His home, that evening
THREE: His office, the next morning

ONE

Gould's office. Morning. Boxes and painting materials all around. Gould is sitting, reading, Fox enters.

GOULD: When the gods would make us mad, they answer our prayers.

FOX: Bob . . .

GOULD: I'm in the midst of the wilderness.

FOX: Bob . . .

GOULD: If it's not quite "Art" and it's not quite "Entertainment," it's here on my desk. I have inherited a monster.

FOX: . . . Bob . . .

GOULD: Listen to this . . . (*Reads:*) "How are things made round? Was there one thing which, originally, was round . . .?"

FOX: . . . Bob . . .

GOULD (*leafing through the book he is reading, reads*): "A certain frankness came to it . . ." (*He leafs.*) "The man,

3

downcast, then met the priest, under the bridge, beneath that bridge which stood for so much, where so much had transpired *since* the radiation."

FOX: . . . yeah, Bob, that's great . . .

GOULD: Listen to this: "and with it brought grace. But still the questions persisted . . . that of the Radiation. That of the growth of animalism, the decay of the soil. And it said 'Beyond terror. Beyond grace' . . . and caused a throbbing . . . machines in the void . . ." (*He offers the book to Fox.*) Here: take a page.

FOX: I have to talk to you.

GOULD: Chuck, Chuck, Chuck, *Charles*: you get too old, too busy to have 'fun' this business; to have 'fun,' then what are you . . .?

FOX: . . . Bob . . .

GOULD: What are you?

FOX: What am I . . .?

GOULD: Yes.

FOX: What am I when?

GOULD: What are you, I was saying, if you're just a slave to commerce?

FOX: If I'm just a slave to commerce?

GOULD: Yes.

FOX: I'm nothing.

GOULD: No.

FOX: You're absolutely right.

GOULD: You got to have fun. You know why?

Fox: Okay: why?

Gould: Because, or else you'll die, and people will say "he never had any fun."

Fox: How close are you to Ross?

Gould: How close am I to Ross . . .? I don't know. How close should I be?

Fox: I have to ask you something.

Gould (*pause*): Go ahead, Charl.

Fox: You wanna' greenlight a picture? What's your deal, what's your new deal?

Gould: What's my new deal, that's all you can talk about?

Fox: What's your new deal?

Gould: Alright. Over ten mil I need Ross's approval. Under ten mil, I can greenlight it. So what. (*Pause.*)

Fox: This morning, Bob.

Gould: . . . Yes . . .?

Fox: This morning a man came to me.

Gould: . . . a man came to you. Whaddayou, already, you're here to "Promote" me . . .?

Fox: Bob . . .

Gould: You here to promote me? Charl? Because, Charl, one thing I don't need . . .

Fox: Bob.

Gould: When everybody in this jolly *town* is tryin' to promote me, do you wanna see my messages . . .?

Fox: Bob.

GOULD: "Get Him While He's Hot" . . .

FOX: Yes, yes, but . . .

GOULD: My good, my "good" friend, Charles Fox . . .

FOX: Bob . . .

GOULD: That's why we have "channels."

FOX: Uh huh.

GOULD: All these "little" people out there, that we see. Y'unnerstand? Fellow asks "what are they *there* for?" Well, Charl, We Don't Know. But we *think*, you give the thing to *your* boy, gives it to *my* boy, these people get to *eat*, they don't have to go *beg*, and get in everybody's face the *airport* the whole time. This morning the phone won't stop ringing. Do you know who's calling? Everybody says they met me in *Topeka*, 1962, and do I want to make their movie. Guys want me to do remakes of films haven't been made yet.

FOX: . . . Huh, huh . . .

GOULD: I'm drowning in "coverage." (*He picks up a script and reads:*) "The Story of a Horse and the Horse Who Loved Him." (*He drops script.*) . . . Give me a breather from all those fine folk suddenly see what a great "man" I am. N'when I *do* return my calls, Charl, do you know what I'll tell those people?

FOX: No.

GOULD: I'm going to tell them "Go through Channels." This protects me from them. And from folk, fine as they are, like you, Charl, when you come to me for favors. Or did you come up here to congratulate me on my new promotion?

FOX: Congratulations.

GOULD: Do I deserve it?

FOX: Yes. You do, Bob.

GOULD: Why?

FOX: Because you're a prince among men and you're Yertle the Turtle.

GOULD: Alright then, that's enough. What did you bring me?

FOX: This morning, Bob.

GOULD: Yes?

FOX: This morning Doug Brown came to me.

GOULD: . . . Doug Brown.

FOX (*pause*): He came to my *house* Bob. How would you *like* . . . How would you like for Doug Brown to "cross the street" to do a picture for us? (*Pause.*) Bob? How would you *like*, a script that I got him. He's *nuts* for it, he's *free*, we could start to shoot next *month*, I have his word and he'll come to the studio, and do the film for us. Doug Brown will cross the street and do a film for us next month.

GOULD (*picks up phone*): Get me Ross. (*Pause.*)

FOX: . . . do you see what I'm telling you?

GOULD: . . . he came to your house . . .

FOX: . . . can you believe what I'm saying to you . . .?

GOULD: Douggie Brown. (*Into phone:*) Ross (*pause*) *Richard Ross* . . . no, no, no, *don't* look in the book . . . there's a button on the console . . . Richard R . . . just push the button on the . . . (*Pause.*) There's a button on the console . . . Richard Ross . . . just . . . *Thank* you. (*Hangs up the phone. Pause.*) Are you alright?

FOX: I'm fine. I'm fine, I just need coffee.

GOULD: We'll get it for you. Tell mmm . . .

FOX: Alright, I, this is some time ago.

GOULD: . . . uh huh . . .

FOX: That I get the script to Brown . . .

GOULD: What script . . .?

FOX: You don't know it, a prison script . . .

GOULD (*simultaneously with "script"*): One of ours . . .?

FOX: I found it in the file. I *loved* it . . . all the time I'm thinking . . .

GOULD: Uh huh . . .

FOX: How to do this script, I, one day . . .

GOULD: Uh huh . . .

FOX: . . . so . . .

GOULD: So, you give the script to Brown . . .

FOX: Not "him," his . . .

GOULD: Uh huh . . .

FOX: . . . his . . .

GOULD: . . . I know . . .

FOX: His "guy."

GOULD: Yes.

FOX: *Gives* Douggie the script . . . (*Phone rings.* GOULD *picks up the phone.*)

GOULD (*into phone*): Yes. Thank you. (*Hangs up.*) Ross'll get back to us . . .

FOX: . . . His guy *gives* Douggie the scri . . .

GOULD: He gives Douggie the script.

FOX: Yes.

GOULD: Mmm . . .

FOX: *Months* ago, alright? *I* don't know. *Today*, alright . . . ? Today. (*Pause.*) I'm having coffee . . .

GOULD: Umm hmmm . . .

FOX: Who drives up?

GOULD: . . . coffee at your house . . .

FOX: Who drives up?

GOULD: Douggie Brown.

FOX: Douglas Brown drives up to my house. (*Pause.*) He says "I Want To Do Your Script. I've got this other thing to deal with, and we'll settle it tomorrow. Call me ten o'clock tomorrow morning. I'll come in and sign *up*." (*Phone rings.*)

GOULD (*into phone*): Hello . . . who? No calls. *No* calls. Just Richard Ross. And we need coffee . . . okay? *Got* it . . . ? (*Hangs up.*)

FOX: . . . cross the street to shoot it . . . ? And he says "why not." (*Pause.*)

GOULD: . . . huh . . .

FOX: *Huh* . . . ?

GOULD: . . . He'd come over here to shoot it . . .

FOX: Sonofabitch like out of some damn fairytale.

GOULD: . . . he drove to your house . . .

FOX: . . . I'm looking out the window . . .

GOULD: . . . son of a bitch . . .

FOX: . . . Douglas Brown drives up . . .

(*The phone rings.* GOULD *picks it up.*)

GOULD (*into phone*): Hello. Yes. *Richard* . . . (*Pause.*) Yes. Put him . . . Hello, *Richard.* Fine, just fine. They're painting it. Well, thank you. Thank you. Listen Richard. Do you need some good news . . .? (*Pause.*) Well, it's a surprise that I've got for you. No, I want to tell you in person. Do you have five mi . . . (*Checks watch.*) We'll be there. (*Pause.*) Charlie Fox . . . *Charlie* came in with a . . . (*Pause.*) Right. Right. We'll be there. Right. (*Hangs up.*) Well. We see him in ten minutes.

FOX: *Yessir.* I need some coffee.

GOULD: Oh, Jesus, what's the . . .

FOX: What . . .?

GOULD: The, what's the story? Tell me the . . .

FOX: *I* can tell it. No, you're right. *You* tell it.

GOULD: Gimme the broad outl . . .

FOX: Yes, yes.

GOULD: Just sketch me the broad . . .

FOX: Yes, yes, the *thing*, of course, is . . .

GOULD: Douggie, Brown, of course, the thing . . .

FOX: "A Douggie Brown picture" . . .

GOULD: A Douggie Brown picture . . .

FOX: Eh? A buddy . . .

GOULD: A *Buddy* Picture.

FOX: Douggie and . . .

GOULD: "Watch this space," I got it . . .

FOX: Right.

GOULD: The Flavor of the Month . . . okay, now, what's the
    story?

FOX: Doug's in prison.

GOULD: . . . prison . . .

FOX: Right. These guys, they want to get him.

GOULD: *Black* guys . . .

FOX: Black guys in the prison.

GOULD (*into phone*): Coffee, quickly, can you get some
    coffee in here? (*Hangs up.*)

FOX: And the black guys going to rape his ass.

GOULD: Mmm.

FOX: Okay. Now. "Now, you could," he goes, "you could
    have your 'way' with me, all of you . . ."

GOULD: Uh huh, what? ten or twenty guys . . .

FOX: ". . . and you could *do* that. But I'd have to, you
    see? Here's the *thing* of it. Unless you *killed* me, I
    would . . ."

GOULD: Uh huh . . .

FOX: ". . . have to come back and *retaliate*, sometime, somehow, because . . ."

GOULD: . . . okay . . .

FOX: "I couldn't . . ."

GOULD: . . . uh huh . . .

FOX: ". . . *live* with that."

GOULD: . . . The degradation . . .

FOX: "So whyn't you skip all the *middle* shit, kill me right now."

GOULD: . . . he throws it in their face.

FOX: You got it.

GOULD: . . . uh huh . . .

FOX: "*Or.*" (*Pause.*) Or . . .

GOULD: . . . yes . . .

FOX: "If you could use a *friend*, why not allow me this? To *be* your friend . . ."

GOULD: He teams up with the guys . . .

FOX: "To *side* with you . . ."

GOULD: Yes.

FOX: "and *together* . . ."

GOULD: . . . and . . .

FOX: . . . they become friends, they teach him the . . .

GOULD: . . . he learns the Prison Ways . . .

FOX: They blah blah, *so* on . . .

GOULD: Uh huh . . .

FOX: *Now.* Eh? Now. With his, his knowledge of *computers*, so on, with his *money* . . .

GOULD: . . . yeah . . .

FOX: His Links to the Outside . . .

GOULD: A girl . . .?

FOX: Ah. Now that's the *great* part, I'm telling you, when I saw this script . . .

GOULD: . . . I don't know how it got past us . . .

FOX: When they get out of *prison*, the Head Convict's Sister . . .

GOULD: . . . a buddy film, a prison film, Douggie Brown, blah, blah, some girl . . .

FOX: Action, a social . . .

GOULD: Action, blood, a social theme . . .

FOX (*simultaneously with "theme"*): That's what I'm *saying*, an offbeat . . .

GOULD: Good. Good. Good. Alright. Now: Now: when we go in . . .

FOX: That's what I'm saying. Bob.

GOULD: Don't even say it.

FOX: Bob:

GOULD: I understand.

FOX: . . . I wanted to say . . .

GOULD: I know what you wanted to say, and you're right. I know what you're going to ask, and I'm going to see you get it. Absolutely right: You go on this package as the co-producer. (*Pause.*) The name above the title. This is your . . .

FOX: . . . thank you . . .

GOULD: *Thank* me?

FOX: Thank you, Bob.

GOULD: *Hey*: You came in here.

FOX: . . . thank you . . .

GOULD: Hey, Charl, it's *right* . . .

FOX: No, but the thing is that you *thought* of it. You thought of me. You thought to *say* it.

GOULD: I should be thanking you and I *do* thank you.

FOX: Thank you, Bob.

GOULD: This is your thing and you should get a bump.

FOX: Thank you.

GOULD: Because. *Charlie*: Don't thank me. You start me off here with a bang. I know that you could have Gone Across the Street . . .

FOX: I wouldn't have done that.

GOULD: But you could.

FOX: I wouldn't . . .

GOULD: But you *could.* And that's the point, Charl. That you absolutely *could.* And it was "loyalty" kept you with us . . .

FOX: Hey, hey, it's only common sense.

GOULD: You stuck with the Home Store.

FOX: Hey, you've been good for me, to put it bluntly, all the years . . .

GOULD: . . . you stuck with the Old Firm, Charl, you stuck with your friends.

FOX: It's where I work, Bob, it's what I *do*, and my relationship with you . . . we were all happy for you, Bob, you got bumped up, and I feel that I'm lucky . . .

GOULD: *I'm* the lucky one, Charl . . .

FOX: Hey, Bullshit, to have somebody I could *come* to . . .

GOULD (*simultaneously with "come"*): Because you *could* have gone Across the Street. Who would have blamed you?

FOX: Yeah, but I wouldn't of done it.

GOULD: Who would of blamed you, Charl? You get a Free Option on a Douggie Brown film, guys would walk in here, hold a guy up . . .

FOX: I work here, Bob. And my loyalty has always been to you. (*Pause.*)

GOULD: Well, I'm one lucky son of a bitch . . .

FOX: That you are.

GOULD: And what I do is "owe you."

FOX: No, no, Bob. Bull*shit* . . . The times you've . . .

GOULD: I'm just doing my job.

FOX: No, I know, I know . . . and I know at times, that it was *difficult* for you . . .

GOULD: No.

FOX: I, and I hesitate to *ask* it, to ask for the credit . . .

GOULD: . . . Don't *have* to ask it.

FOX: 'Cause I know, anybody was to *come* in here, *exploit* you . . . this thing . . .

GOULD: . . . *Forget* . . .

FOX: . . . your new "position," all, I even hesitate . . .

GOULD: Don't hesitate about a goddamn thing, *forget* it, Charl: *You Brought Me Gold.* You're gonna be co-producer. What the fuck are you *talkin'* about . . .?

FOX: I just, I wanted to say . . .

GOULD (*simultaneously with "say"*): I'm grateful to *you*, pal. For *this* n'for all that you've been, over the years . . .

FOX: Now . . . *you* know . . .

GOULD: Hey, hey, hey (GOULD *checks his watch.*) Let's go make some money. (*He rises.*)

FOX: I, I need a cuppa coffee . . .

GOULD: You get it in Ross's office. Here's how we play it: we get *in* . . .

FOX: . . . yes . . .

GOULD: We get in, get out and we give it to him *in one sentence.* Let *me* talk, no disrespect . . .

FOX: No.

GOULD: But it's courtesy . . .

FOX: I understand.

GOULD: One sentence. "Doug Brown, Buddy Film." (*Phone rings. Into phone:*) Whoever it is, we'll be with Mr. Rrr ... (*Pause.*) Yes? Put him on ... Hello: *Richard.* ... Yes ...? Yes, well, how long will you bbb ... (*Pause.*) I see ... Absolutely. (*Pause.*) No problem whatsoever ... you'll be *back* by then ...? (*Pause.*) Absolutely so. Thank you. (*He hangs up. Pause. To Fox:*) Ross just got called to New York. He's going on the Gulfstream, turn around and come right back. So we got pushed to tomorrow morning, ten o'clock.

FOX (*pause*): *Aha.* (*Pause.*)

GOULD: No help for it.

FOX: I've got, Douggie only gave me until ...

GOULD: ... I'm sorry ...

FOX: Doug Brown only gave me until ten tomorrow morn ...

GOULD: No, I know, we've only got 'til ten to tie ...

FOX: We got to come up with a Pay or Play to *tie* him to this thing by ten o'clock to ...

GOULD: No problem. Ross'll be back for tomorrow morning, if he *doesn't* ...

FOX: ... if he doesn't ...

GOULD: ... yes ...

FOX: ... then ...

GOULD: ... Then we'll raise him on the *phone* ...

FOX: ... I'm saying ...

GOULD: Wherever he is, we'll pull him *out* of *it* ...

Fox: Wherever he is.

Gould: Yup.

Fox: Because I only got the option until ten o'clock tomorrow. Doug Brown told me . . .

Gould: Yeah. I'm *saying*. Ten o'clock tomorrow. Ross: he'll be here, one chance in a *quillion* he isn't, then we go Condition Red, we get him on the . . .

Fox: . . . because . . .

Gould: Yeah, yeah, yeah, I'm *with* you.

Fox: Be . . .

Gould: . . . You understand . . . I wanted to do . . .

Fox: . . . I understand . . .

Gould: I wanted to do it in *person* . . .

Fox: Yes.

Gould: . . . 'Cause you're gonna be the Bringer of Good *News* . . .

Fox: No, no, you're absolutely right.

Gould: Do it in *person* . . .

Fox: . . . yes . . .

Gould: And forge that bond.

Fox: It's just . . .

Gould: Don't worry.

Fox: Not me. It's just, you move up to *the big league* . . . (*Pause.*)

Gould: Charlie. Your ship has come in . . .

FOX (*pause*): . . . all I'm saying . . . *Ross* . . .

GOULD: What's Ross going to say . . . "No"? It's *done*.

FOX: Lord, I believe, aid thou my unbelief . . . the sucker walked in, said "I love the script."

GOULD: Oh yes, Charlie, for we're now the *Fair*-haired boys.

FOX: I couldn't believe it, you talk, talk about, talk, what is the . . . "watersheds."

GOULD: That's right.

FOX: And, that is one of them.

GOULD: And why *shouldn't* it be—you understand . . .?

FOX: *I* don't know.

GOULD: 'Cause you . . .

FOX: . . . I, I don't know . . .

GOULD: . . . You *worked* for it . . . you know, you know . . .

FOX: "I'm going to be rich and I can't believe it."

GOULD: Rich, are you kidding me? We're going to have to hire someone just to figure out the *things* we want to buy . . .

FOX: I mean, I mean, you think about a concept, all your life . . .

GOULD: . . . I'm with you . . .

FOX: "Wealth."

GOULD: Yes. Wealth.

FOX: Then it comes *down* to you . . .

GOULD: Uh huh . . .

FOX: All you can think of . . . "*This* is what that means . . ."

GOULD: And that *is* what it means. (*Pause.*)

FOX: How, how, figuring up the rentals, tie in, foreign, air, the . . .

GOULD: Uh huh . . .

FOX: Over the course . . .

GOULD: . . . don't forget the sequels.

FOX: Do we . . . we're tied in to that . . .?

GOULD: Are we tied in to that, Charl? Welcome to the world.

FOX: Hhhhh. How . . . (*Pause.*)

GOULD: The question, your crass question: how much money could we stand to make . . .?

FOX: Yes.

GOULD: I think the operative concept here is "lots and lots . . ."

FOX: Oh, maan . . .

GOULD: Great big jolly *shitloads* of it.

FOX: Oh, maan . . .

GOULD: But money . . .

FOX: Yeah.

GOULD: Money, Charl . . .

FOX: Yeah . . .

GOULD: Money is not the important thing.

FOX: No.

GOULD: Money is not Gold.

FOX: No.

GOULD: What can you do with Money?

FOX: Nothing.

GOULD: Nary a goddamn thing.

FOX: . . . I'm gonna be rich.

GOULD: "Buy" things with it.

FOX: Where would I *keep* them?

GOULD: What would you *do* with them?

FOX: Yeah.

GOULD: Take them out and *dust* them, time to time.

FOX: Oh yeah.

GOULD: I piss on money.

FOX: I know that you do. I'll help you.

GOULD: *Fuck* money.

FOX: Fuck it. Fuck "things" too . . .

GOULD: Uh huh. But don't fuck "people."

FOX: No.

GOULD: 'Cause, people, Charlie . . .

FOX: People . . . yes.

GOULD: Are what it's All About.

FOX: I know.

GOULD: And it's a People Business.

FOX: That it is.

GOULD: It's *full* of fucken' people . . .

FOX: And we're gonna kick some ass, Bob.

GOULD: That we are.

FOX: We're gonna kick the ass of a lot of them fucken' people.

GOULD: That's right.

FOX: We get rolling, Bob. It's "up the ass with gun and camera."

GOULD: Yup.

FOX: 'Cause when you spend twenty years in the barrel . . .

GOULD: . . . I know . . .

FOX: No, you *don't* know, you've forgotten. Due respect.

GOULD: . . . may be . . .

FOX: But, but . . . oh maan . . . I'm gonna settle some fucken' scores.

GOULD: Better things to do . . .

FOX: If there are, *show* them to me, man . . . A bunch of cocksuckers out there. Gimme' a cigarette. Oh, Man, I can't come down.

GOULD: No need to. Huh . . .?

FOX: Ross, Ross, Ross isn't going to fuck me out of this . . .?

GOULD: No. Absolutely not. You have my word.

FOX: I don't need your word, Bob. I know *you* . . . Drives right to my house. I need a cup of coffee.

GOULD (*into phone*): Could we get a cup . . . well, where did you try? Why not try the *coffee mach* . . . well, it's right down at the . . . down the, no, it's unmarked, just go . . . that's right. (*Hangs up.*)

FOX: What, you got a new broad, go with the new job . . .

GOULD: No. Cathy's just out sick.

FOX: Cute broad, the new broad.

GOULD: What? She's cute? The broad out there is cute? Baby, she's nothing. You wait 'til we make this film.

FOX: She's nothing?

GOULD: Playing in this league? I'm saying, it's Boy's Choice: Skate in One Direction Only. (*Pause.*)

FOX: Oh, man, what am I going to *do* today?

GOULD: Go to a movie, get your hair done.

FOX: I'm jumping like a leaf.

GOULD: It's a done deal. We walk in *tomorrow* . . .

FOX (*picks up the book*): What's this, what's the thing you're reading I come in?

GOULD: This thing?

FOX: Uh huh . . .

GOULD: From the East. An Eastern Sissy Writer. (*Passes the book to* FOX.)

FOX (*reads*): "The Bridge: or, Radiation and the Half-Life of Society. A Study of Decay."

GOULD: A Novel.

FOX: Great.

GOULD: A cover note from Richard Ross: "Give this a Courtesy Read."

FOX (*reads*): "The wind against the Plains, but not a wind of change . . . a wind like that one which he'd been foretold, the rubbish of the world—swirling, swirling . . . two thousand years . . ." Hey I wouldn't just give it a *courtesy* read, I'd *make* this sucker.

GOULD: Good idea.

FOX: Drop a dime on western civilization.

GOULD: . . . 'Bout time.

FOX: Why don't you do that? *Make* it.

GOULD: I think that I will.

FOX: Yeah. Instead of our Doug, Doug Brown's *Buddy* film.

GOULD: Yeah. *I* could do that. You know why? Because my job, my new job is one thing: the capacity to make decisions.

FOX: I know that it is.

GOULD: Decide, decide, decide . . .

FOX: It's lonely at the top.

GOULD: But it ain't crowded.

(KAREN, *the secretary, comes in with a tray of coffee.*)

KAREN: I'm sorry, please, but how do you take your coffee . . .?

FOX: He takes his coffee like he makes his movies: nothing in it.

GOULD: Very funny.

FOX: 'Cause he's an Old Whore.

GOULD: . . . that's right . . .

FOX: Bobby Gould . . .

GOULD: . . . Huh . . .

FOX: You're just an Old Whore.

GOULD: Proud of it. Yes, yes.

FOX: They kick you upstairs and you're still just some old whore.

GOULD: You're an old whore, too.

FOX: I never said I wasn't. Soon to be a *rich* old whore.

GOULD: That's right.

FOX: And I deserve it.

GOULD: That you do, Babe, that you do.

FOX: Because, Miss, lemme tell you something, I've been *loyal* to this guy, you know, you know . . . *what's* your name?

KAREN: Karen . . .

FOX: Karen, lemme tell you: since the *mail* room . . . you know? Step-by-step. Yes, in his shadow, yes, why not. Never forgot him, and he never forgot me.

GOULD: That's absolutely right.

FOX: You know why I never forgot him?

KAREN: . . . I . . .

FOX: . . . Because the shit of his I had to eat, how *could* I forget him?

GOULD: . . . huh . . .

FOX: Yes, but the Wheel Came Around. And here we are. Two Whores. (*To* GOULD:) You're gonna decorate your office. Make it a bordello. You'll feel more at home.

GOULD: *You*, you sonofabitch . . .

FOX: . . . and come to work in a soiled nightgown.

GOULD: Hey, after the Doug Brown thing, I come to work in that same nightgown, I say "kiss the hem," then every swinging dick in this man's studio will kiss that hem.

FOX: They will.

GOULD: They'll *french* that jolly jolly hem.

FOX: Uh huh, uh huh . . . *you*, you, you fucken' whore, on his deathbed, St. Peter'll come for him, his dying words, "Just let me turn One More Trick . . ."

GOULD: I'm a whore and I'm proud of it. But I'm a *secure* whore. Yes, and you get *ready*, now: you get ready 'cause they're going to plot, they're going to plot against you . . . (*To* KAREN:) Karen. My friend's stepping up in class . . . (*To* FOX:) They're going to plot against you, Charlie, like they plotted against me. They're going to go back in their Tribal Caves and say "Chuck Fox, that *hack* . . ."

FOX: "That powerful hack . . ."

GOULD: Let's go and steal his job . . .

KAREN: Sir . . . ?

FOX: Black, two sugars, thank you.

GOULD: To your face they'll go, "Three bags full." And behind your back they'll say, "let's tear him down— let's tear Charlie Fox down . . ."

FOX: Behind my back. Yes, but in Public . . . ? They'll say: "I waxed Mr. Fox's car. He seemed pleased."

KAREN (*serving coffee*): Black, two sugars.

FOX: "I blew his poodle. He gave me a smile." (*Of coffee:*) Thank you.

GOULD: This is Charlie Fox. This is . . . *Karen* . . .

FOX: Yes. Good morning.

KAREN: Good morning, sir.

GOULD: Please put me down. Tomorrow. Richard Ross. His office. Ten A.M. Whatever you find in the book, call back and *cancel* it. And leave a note for Cathy, should she be back . . .

KAREN: I'm told that she'll be back tomorrow.

GOULD: . . . draw her attention to our meeting with Ross.

KAREN: Yessir.

FOX: Karen, as Mr. Gould moves on up the ladder, will you go with him?

KAREN: Sir?

FOX: When . . .

KAREN: I'm just a temporary . . .

GOULD: That's right, she's just here for a . . .

Fox: Well, would you like stay on, if ... ?

Gould: Hey, what are you? The Master of the Revels?

Karen: I'm just, I'm on a temporary ...

Fox: Hey, everything's temporary 'til it's "not" ...

Karen: No, this is just a temporary job.

Gould: It's just a temporary job—so leave the girl alone.

Fox: Karen: yeah: Karen, this seem like a good place to work?

Karen: Sir?

Fox: Call me Charlie. This seem like a good place to work?

Karen: Here?

Fox: Mr. Gould's office.

Karen: I'm sure that it is.

Fox: She's "sure that it is." How wonderful to be so sure. How wonderful to have such certainty in this wonderful world. Hey, Bobby ... ? Your boss tells you "take initiative," you best guess right—and you *do*, then you get no credit. Day-in, ... smiling, smiling, just a cog.

Gould: Mr. Fox is talking about his own self.

Fox: You *bet* I am. But my historical self, Bob, for I am a cog no more.

Gould: Karen, you come here at an auspicious time.

Fox: *Give* this man a witness.

Gould: Because in this sinkhole of slime and depravity, something is about to work out.

FOX: . . . singing a song, rolling along.

GOULD: . . . and all that garbage that we put up with is going to pay off. (*Pause.*)

KAREN: . . . why is it garbage . . .? (*Pause.*)

GOULD: It's not all garbage, but most of it is.

KAREN: Why?

GOULD: Why. That's a good . . . (*To* FOX:) Why? (*Pause.*)

FOX: Because.

GOULD (*to* KAREN): Because.

FOX: Life in the movie business is like the, is like the beginning of a new love affair: it's full of surprises, and you're constantly getting fucked.

KAREN: But why should it all be garbage?

FOX: Why? Why should nickels be bigger than dimes? That's the way it is.

GOULD: It's a business, with its own unchanging rules. Isn't that right, Charlie?

FOX: Yes, it is. The *one* thing is: nobody pays off on work.

GOULD: That is the truth.

FOX: Everybody says "Hey, I'm a maverick."

GOULD: That's it . . .

FOX: But what do they do? Sit around like, hey, Pancho-the-dead-whale . . .

GOULD: . . . huh . . .

FOX: Waiting for the . . .

GOULD: . . . mmm . . .

FOX: Yeah . . .? The Endorsement of their Superiors . . .

GOULD: Uh huh. Listen to the guy. He's telling you.

FOX: You wanna *do* something out here, it better be one of The Five Major Food Groups.

GOULD: Uh huh.

FOX: Or your superiors go napsy—bye. The *upside* of which, though, a guy . . .

GOULD: . . . that's right . . .

FOX: The *upside* . . .

GOULD: Hmm.

FOX: The *upside*, though . . .

GOULD: . . . Hmm.

FOX: The one time you *do* get support . . .

GOULD: . . . hey . . .

FOX: If you *do* have a relationship . . .

GOULD: Hey, Charl, kidding aside, that is what I'm here for . . .

FOX: Then, you can do something. (*To* KAREN, *of Gould*:) This guy, Karen, this guy . . . the last eleven years.

GOULD: *Forget* it . . .

FOX: Forget? Bullshit. This man, my friend . . .

GOULD: Now we're even.

FOX: Oh, you Beauty . . . What's it like being Head of Production? I mean, is it more fun than miniature golf?

GOULD: You put as much energy in your job as you put into kissing my ass . . .

FOX: My job *is* kissing your ass.

GOULD And don't you forget it.

FOX: Not a chance. (*Pause.*)

KAREN: Sir:

GOULD: Yes.

KAREN (*pause*): I feel silly saying it.

GOULD: What?

KAREN: I . . .

GOULD: Well, whatever it is, say it.

KAREN (*pause*): I don't know what to do. (*Pause.*) I don't know what I'm supposed to do. (*Pause.*)

GOULD: Well, that was very frank of you. I tell you what: don't do anything.

KAREN: Sir . . .?

GOULD: We'll call it a Bank Holiday. (*To* FOX:) Huh? Let's get out of here.

FOX: Good, let's get out of here.

GOULD: Huh?

FOX: Well done.

GOULD: And let's get out of here. (*To* KAREN:) Look in my book, and *cancel* whatever I've got today. Anybody calls, call me tomorrow. I'll be in tomorrow for my ten A.M. meeting with Ross.

FOX: Young America at WORK and PLAY.

GOULD: You get done cancelling my stuff, you can go home.

FOX: Where we going for lunch?

GOULD: Well, I figured we'd drop by the commissary, get the tuna sandwich, then go swishing by Laura Ashley and pick out some cunning prints for my new office.

FOX: Whyn't you just paint it with broken capillaries, decorate it like the inside of your nose.

GOULD: I may. I just may. So, lunch, the Coventry, in half an hour. (*To* KAREN:) Call the Coventry. Table for two, at One. Thank you. (*She exits. Pause. He sighs.*) First in war. First in peace. First in the hearts of Pee Wee Reese.

FOX: Lunch at the Coventry.

GOULD: That's right.

FOX: Thy will be done.

GOULD: You see, all that you got to do is eat my doo doo for eleven years, and eventually the wheel comes round.

FOX: Pay back time.

GOULD: You brought me the Doug Brown script.

FOX: Glad I could do it.

GOULD: You son of a *bitch* . . .

FOX: Hey.

GOULD: Charl, I just hope.

FOX: What?

GOULD: The shoe was on the other foot, I'd act in such a . . .

FOX: . . . hey . . .

GOULD: Really, princely way toward *you*.

FOX: I *know* you would, Bob, because lemme tell you: experiences like this, *films* like this . . . these are the films . . .

GOULD: . . . Yes . . .

FOX: *These* are the films, that whaddayacallit . . . (*long pause*) that make it all worthwhile.

GOULD: . . . I think you're going to find a *lot* of things now, make it all worthwhile. I think *conservatively*, you and me, we build ourselves in to split, minimally, ten percent. (*Pause.*)

FOX: Of the net.

GOULD: Char, Charlie: permit me to tell you: two things I've learned, twenty-five years in the entertainment industry.

FOX: What?

GOULD: The two things which are always true.

FOX: One:

GOULD: The first one is: there is no net.

FOX: Yeah . . .? (*Pause.*)

GOULD: And I forgot the second one. Okay, I'm gonna meet you at the Coventry in half an hour. We'll talk about boys and clothes.

FOX: Whaddaya gonna do the interim?

GOULD: I'm gonna *Work* . . . (*Indicating his figures on the pad.*)

Fox: Work . . .? You never did a day's work in your life.

Gould: Oooh, Oooh, . . . the Bitching Lamp is Lit.

Fox: You never did a fucken' day's work in your life.

Gould: That true?

Fox: Eleven years I've known you, you're either scheming or you're ziggin' and zaggin', hey, I *know* you, Bob.

Gould: Oh yes, the scorn of the impotent . . .

Fox: I know you, Bob. I know you from the *back*. *I* know what you're staying for.

Gould: You do?

Fox: Yes.

Gould: What?

Fox: You're staying to Hide the Afikomen.

Gould: Yeah?

Fox: You're staying to put those moves on your new secretary.

Gould: I am?

Fox: Yeah, and it *will* not work.

Gould: It will not work, what are you saying . . .?

Fox: No, I was just saying that she . . .

Gould: . . . she wouldn't go for me.

Fox: That she won't go for you.

Gould (*pause*): Why?

Fox: Why? (*Pause.*) I don't know.

GOULD: What do you see . . .?

FOX: I think . . . I think . . . you serious?

GOULD: Yes.

FOX: I don't want to pee on your parade.

GOULD: No . . .

FOX: I mean, I'm sorry that I took the edge off it.

GOULD: I wasn't *going* to hit on her.

FOX: Hmmm.

GOULD: I was gonna . . .

FOX: You were gonna work.

GOULD: Yes.

FOX: Oh.

GOULD (*pause*): But tell me what you see.

FOX: What I see, what I *saw*, just an observation . . .

GOULD: . . . yes . . .

FOX: It's not important.

GOULD: Tell me what you see. Really.

FOX: I just thought, I just thought she falls between two stools.

GOULD: And what would those stools be?

FOX: That she is not, just some, you know, a "floozy" . . .

GOULD: A "floozy" . . .

FOX: . . . on the other hand, I think I'd have to say, I don't think she is so *ambitious* she would schtup you just to get ahead. (*Pause.*) That's all. (*Pause.*)

GOULD: What if she just "liked" me? (*Pause.*)

FOX: If she just "liked" you?

GOULD: Yes.

FOX: Ummm. (*Pause.*)

GOULD: Yes.

FOX: You're saying, if she just . . . *liked* you . . . (*Pause.*)

GOULD: You mean nobody loves me for myself.

FOX: No.

GOULD: No?

FOX: Not in *this* office . . .

GOULD: And she's neither, what, vacant nor ambitious enough to go . . .

FOX: . . . I'm not saying you don't *deserve* it, you *do* deserve it. Hey, . . . I think you're worth it.

GOULD: Thank you. You're saying that she's neither, what, dumb, nor ambitious enough, she would go to bed with me.

FOX: . . . she's too, she's too . . .

GOULD: She's too . . . High-line . . .?

FOX: No, she's, she's too . . .

GOULD: She's too . . .

FOX: . . . yes.

GOULD: Then what's she doing in this office?

FOX: She's a *Temporary* Worker.

GOULD: You're full of it, Chuck.

FOX: Maybe. And I didn't mean to take the *shine* off our . . .

GOULD: Hey, hey, he sends the cross, he sends the strength to bear it. Go to, go to lunch, I'll meet you at . . .

FOX: I didn't mean to imply . . .

GOULD: Imply. Naaa. Nobody Loves Me. Nobody loves me for myself. Hey, Big Deal, don't go mopin' on me here. We'll go and celebrate. A Douglas Brown Film. Fox and Gould . . .

FOX: . . . you're very kind . . .

GOULD: . . . you brought the guy in. Fox and Gould Present:

FOX: I'll see you at lunch . . . (*Starts to exit.*)

GOULD: But I bet she would go, I bet she *would* go out with me.

FOX: I bet she would, too.

GOULD: No, No. I'm saying, I think that she "likes" me.

FOX: Yeah. I'm sure she does.

GOULD: No, joking apart, Babe. My *perceptions* . . . Say I'm nuts, I don't *think* so—she likes me, and she'd go out with me.

FOX: How much?

GOULD: How much? Seriously . . .? (*Pause.*)

FOX: Yeah.

GOULD: . . . that she would . . .?

FOX: Yeah. That she would *anything*. (*Pause.*) That she would anything. (*Pause.*) That she would deal with you in any other than a professional way. (*Pause.*)

GOULD: Well, my, my, my, my, my.

FOX: What can I tell you, "*Bob.*"

GOULD: That I can get her on a date, that I can get her to my house, that I can screw her.

FOX: I don't think so.

GOULD: How much? (*Pause.*)

FOX: A hundred bucks.

GOULD: That's enough?

FOX: Five hundred bucks that you can't.

GOULD: Five hundred? That's enough?

FOX: A gentleman's bet.

GOULD: Done. Now get out of here, and let me work . . . the Coventry at One. I need . . .

FOX: The script, the budget, chain of ownership . . .

GOULD: Good.

FOX: I'll swing by my, I'll bring it to lunch.

GOULD: Good. Char . . . (*Pause.*)

FOX: What?

GOULD: Thank you.

FOX: Hey. Fuck you. (*Exits.*)

(GOULD *sits alone for a moment, writing.* KAREN *enters.*)

KAREN: Mr. Gould . . .

GOULD: Bobby.

KAREN: Sir. (*Pause.*) I was not able to get you a table at the Coventry. But I tentatively booked you at . . .

GOULD: Whoa, whoa, whoa, whoa. (*Pause.*) It's alright. I'm going to tell you what you did, and it's alright you did it. Sit down. You called up the Coventry and asked them for a table for two at one o'clock. And they told you they had absolutely nothing. That right?

KAREN: Yes. (*Pause.*) I . . . I . . . I'm so sorry. Of course. I should have mentioned your name.

GOULD: It's alright.

KAREN: It was very . . . it was *naïve* of me.

GOULD: It's alright.

KAREN: I had . . . no: you're right. I had a thought, when I was hanging up, then I thought: "You forgot to . . ."

GOULD: . . . it's alright.

KAREN: "You forgot to 'tell' them," then I thought: "what difference does it make? If they don't have a *table* . . ."

GOULD: It's alright.

KAREN: If they didn't have a table, what difference who called up? But, of *course*, they have a table for *you* . . . I'm sorry. It was naïve of me.

GOULD: Listen, there's nothing wrong with being naïve, with learning . . .

KAREN (*simultaneously with "learning"*): And I'm sure . . . I'm sorry.

GOULD: No, go on.

KAREN: . . . I was going to say . . .

GOULD: . . . yes . . .?

KAREN: I was going to say that I'm sure that much of a job like this, a job like this, is learning to think in a . . .

GOULD: Yes.

KAREN: To think in a . . . business fashion.

GOULD: That's what makes the life exciting, *addictive*, *you* know what I'm talking about, you want a *thrill* in your life?

KAREN: . . . a thrill . . .?

GOULD: To *make* something, to *do* something, to be a *part* of something. Money, art, a chance to Play at the Big Table . . . Hey, you're here, and you want to participate in it. (*Pause.*)

KAREN: Yes.

GOULD: Well, of course you do. And it *is* an exciting world.

KAREN: I'm sure it is.

GOULD: Sudden changes all the time. You want to *know* some of it. Now, you want to know a secret?

KAREN: Yes.

GOULD: I'll *tell* you one. Siddown. (KAREN *sits.*) Charlie Fox comes in and he's formed a relationship with Doug Brown. Doug will leave his studio and do a film with us. Charlie Fox brought it to us, brought it to *me* really. And in the Highest Traditions of the Motion Picture Industry, we're actually going to make a movie.

KAREN: Is it a good film?

GOULD: I'm sorry.

KAREN: Is it a good film?

GOULD: Well, it's a commodity. And I admire you for not being ashamed to ask the question. Yes, it's a good question, and I don't *know* if it is a good film. "What about Art?" I'm not an artist. Never said I was, and nobody who sits in this chair can be. I'm a businessman. "Can't we try to make good films?" Yes. We try. I'm going to try to make a good film of this prison film. The question: Is there such a thing as a good film which loses money? In general, of course. But, really, not. For *me*, 'cause if the films I make lose money, then I'm back on the streets with a sweet and silly smile on my face, they lost money 'cause nobody saw them, it's my fault. A tree fell in the forest, what did I accomplish? Yes. You *see*? There is a way things are. Some people are elected, try to change the world, this job is not that job. Somebody, somebody . . . in this job, in the job I have, somebody is always trying to "promote" you: to use *something*, some "hook" to get you to do something in their own best interest. You follow me?

KAREN: Of course.

GOULD: 'Cause this *desk* is a position to *advance*, y'understand? It's a *platform* to *aid*, to push someone along. But I Can't *Do* It. Why? That's not my business. My business is to make decisions for the studio. Means I have to be *blunt*, to say "no," much, most of the time, that's my job. And I think it's a *good* job: 'cause it's a job of *responsibility*. Pressure, many rewards. *One* of them, one time in a billion years, someone was loyal to me, and I'm talking about Charlie Fox, stuck *with* me, comes in here, let's face it, does a favor for me . . . he could of took the script across the street, no, but he came to me, now—I can throw in with him and we rise together. That's what the job is. It's a job, all the bullshit aside, deals with *people*. (*He hunts on his desk, picks up a copy of the book he was reading from earlier.*) Look here. Agent gives his client's book to Ross: "The Bridge or, Radiation and the Half-Life of Society": Now, *who* is Mister Ross, now . . .?

KAREN: He is the Head of the Studio.

GOULD: And he has a button on my console. That's right. Author's agent gave this book to Ross. A novel. Written by a Very Famous Eastern Writer. What's this book about? "The End of the World." Great. Now: Ross, no dummy, says, of course, he'll read the book. Gives *me* the book to read, so when he tells the author "how he loved the book but it won't make a movie," he can say something intelligent about it. You get it? This, in the business, is called "a courtesy read."

KAREN: A courtesy read.

GOULD: Yes. No one has any intention of making the book, but we read it, as a courtesy. Does this mean that we're depraved? No. It's just business . . . how business is done, you see?

KAREN: I think.

GOULD: A business. Start to close.

KAREN: But what if there is something in the book?

GOULD: In the book?

KAREN: Yes. (*Pause.*)

GOULD: It's a novel about the historical effects of radiation . . .

KAREN: Yes, but . . .

GOULD: I mean, I mean, the author's crazy as a fucken' June bug.

KAREN: But, but.

GOULD: . . . what if . . .?

KAREN: Yes.

GOULD: What if, after everything . . .

KAREN: . . . yes . . .

GOULD: Hope against hope, there is *something* in the book.

KAREN: Yes.

GOULD: *Something* in the book, that . . .

KAREN: Yes. (*Pause.*)

GOULD: Well, I'd be delighted. No. You're right. You're right. I'll tell you. (*Pause.*) You're making my point. Absolutely. This job corrupts you. You start to think, all the time "what do these people want from me?" (*Pause.*) And everything becomes a task. (*Pause.*)

KAREN: Does it have to be that?

GOULD: Can we keep ourselves pure? Hey, I prayed to be pure.

KAREN: You prayed? To be pure?

GOULD: I did, I said God give me the job as Head of Production. Give me a platform to be "good," and I'll be good. They gave me the job, I'm here one day and *look* at me: a Big Fat Whore. A book, it may be a *fine, fine* book by a well-respected writer. And because this writer's got the reputation being "artsy" . . . artsy, you understand . . . I'm ready, everybody backs me up in this, to assume that his book is unsuitable for the screen, so I look on it as a "courtesy read."

KAREN: Do you enjoy your work?

GOULD: Excuse me?

KAREN: Do, if I'm being too frank . . .

GOULD: . . . do I enjoy my work? Yes. Very much. (*Pause.*) Don't you think *you* would enjoy it?

KAREN: Yes, I think I would enjoy it.

GOULD: You do? Good for you. What of it would you enjoy?

KAREN: The making decisions.

GOULD: Then good for you.

KAREN: Because . . .

GOULD: . . . yes . . .?

KAREN: Perhaps I'm naïve, but I would think that if you could keep your values straight, if you had *principles* to *refer* to, then . . .

GOULD: Hmmm.

KAREN: I know it's naïve . . .

GOULD: Yes it is naïve, and it's also correct.

KAREN: You think it is?

GOULD: Yes, I do. Now, we could talk about purity or we could turn the page. What do you want to do?

KAREN: Talk about purity.

GOULD: Okay. (*Pause.*) If you don't have *principles*, whatever they are . . . then each day is hell, you haven't got

a compass. All you've got is "good taste"; and you can
shove good taste up your ass and fart "The Carnival of
Venice." Good taste will not hack it. 'Cause each day
the pressure just gets worse. It gets more difficult.
(*Pause.*) I want you to do me a favor. Read that book
for me.

KAREN: *I* should read it . . .?

GOULD: Yes.

KAREN: The Radiation Book?

GOULD: Let's be frank: it's probably, it's almost definitely
unsuitable, it probably *is* artsy. But as you said, maybe
it isn't. *You* read it, you'll tell me, and I'll tell Mr.
Ross.

KAREN: . . . I . . .

GOULD: . . . and then, you're right, and then at least we
looked.

KAREN: I'd be flattered to read it.

GOULD: *Good.*

KAREN: Thank you.

GOULD: Not at all. I thank *you.* I'll need a report on it . . .

KAREN: . . . of course.

GOULD: By tonight. How long will it take you to . . .

KAREN: Well, I won't be able to start reading it 'til after
work . . .

GOULD (*simultaneously with "work"*): Fine. Tonight, I'm
going to be home. When you're finished, you bring the
report to me and we'll discuss it.

KAREN: Absolutely. Thank you.

GOULD: Not at all. Now, I've ... Please call the Coventry. Tell them, a table for Mr. Fox and me, twenty minutes ...

KAREN: Yes, I will.

GOULD: I'm going to clean up here before I go. Call Mr. Fox's girl up on the phone, get her to *page* him or to try him in the car.

KAREN: Uh huh.

GOULD: ... and tell him that I'll be ten minutes late.

KAREN: Of course ...

GOULD: ... and tell him he owes me five hundred bucks.

TWO

Gould's apartment. Night. GOULD *and* KAREN. KAREN *is
reading from the book.*

KAREN : He puts his hand on the child's chest, and he says
"heal," as if he felt he had the power to heal him, he
calls on God . . . it's in here . . . something to the effect
that if *ever* in his life he had the power, any power,
that now is the time . . . list . . . (*She reads:*) ". . . in that
lonely place, the low place, the tramp, under the
bridge, he finds him. Faced with his troubles, and
pours out his heart." We hear the rain, and we see,
in his misery, it is forgotten, wet, cold . . . and the
problems which assaulted him: *they do not disap-
pear*, but they are forgotten. He says: years later: it did
not occur to him 'til then that this was happiness.
That the thing which he lacked, he says, was *courage*.
What does the Tramp say? "All fears are one fear. Just
the fear of death. And we accept it, then we are at
peace." And so, you see, and so all of the *events* . . . the
stone, the *instrument*, the *child* which he met, *led*
him there.

GOULD: They led him.

KAREN: . . . in his . . . yes, you see—I know that you see—
and that's, that's to me, that's the perfection of the
story, when I *read* it . . . I almost, I wanted to sit, I saw,
I almost couldn't come to you, the *weight* of it . . .
(*Pause.*) You know what I mean. He says that the
radiation . . . *all* of it, the planes, the televisions,
clocks, all of it *is to the one end*. To *change* us—to, to
bring about a change—all radiation has been sent by
God. To change us. Constantly.

GOULD: To change us.

KAREN: Yes.

GOULD: How?

KAREN: To this new thing. And that we needn't feel frightened. That it comes from God. And I felt empowered.
(*Pause.*) Empowered. (*Pause.*)

GOULD: Empowered . . .

KAREN: You've felt that, I hope you've felt that, when
something made sense, you'd heard it for the longest
time and finally you, you know what it means. So . . .
so . . . it's not *courage*, it's *greater* than courage. Perhaps it *is* courage. You've felt like that.

GOULD: I have.

KAREN: Yes.

GOULD: Felt like . . .

KAREN: Like they say in *stories*: where, where one thing
changes you.

GOULD: . . . have I felt like that? I don't know.

KAREN: . . . and that it puts you at Peace. And I'll tell you:
like books you find at an Inn, or in a bookshop, when,

you know, when you go in, that you'll *find* something there, something. Old, or, or scraps of *paper* . . . have you had this . . .? In a pocket, or, or even on the ground, a phrase . . . something that *changes* you. And you were drawn to it. *Just* like the man. Beneath the bridge. "What was it that you feared?" he says "*Embrace* it . . ." Well! (*Pause.*) And like my coming here. Why? A temporary job. But I thought, who can say I knew, but I thought I knew, I thought: I would find something. (*Pause.*) Too much. It all came at once. So much. May I have another drink? (GOULD *pours drink.*) Do you know, and he says, the *radiation,* in all things: not just in bombs, in microwaves, in *power,* in *air* travel . . . and the *purpose* of this radia-tion . . . well, I've *said* it . . .

GOULD: Thank you.

Karen: No, I thank *you.* Do you know what he's talking about? Fear. A life lived in fear, and he says, It Says In The Book, it doesn't have to *be* so; that those things we have *seen* . . . *you* know, and you think "I, am I the only one on the whole planet who knows how *bad* it is . . . that it's *coming* . . . that it's sure to come." What . . . don't you see? What can I do . . .? And you *can't* join a convent, or "cut off your hair," or, or, or, you see, this is our pain, I think, we *can't* embrace Jesus. *He,* you see, and he says, "I know. And you don't have to be afraid." And I realized: I haven't *breathed.* How long? In *years.* From, I don't know. From terror, perhaps ever. And you say, how can you say it? Is our life so bad? No. No. But that it's ending. That our life is ending. Yes. It's true. And he says that, that these are the Dark Ages. (*Pause.*) They aren't to come, the Dark Ages—they are now. We're living them. (*Reads:*) "In the waning days . . . in the last days" . . . "Yes," he says, it's *true*, and you needn't deny it . . . and I felt such *fear*, because, of course, he's right. Then he says: "do not be afraid." The story . . . when you, when you read it, the story itself. Down below the bridge, I'll tell you: written with such love . . . (*Pause.*) *Such* love . . . (*Pause.*) God. A thing to be thankful for. Such love.

GOULD: You've done a fantastic job.

KAREN: I have?

GOULD: Yes.

KAREN: I have? Doing what?

GOULD: On the book. (*Pause.*)

KAREN: I . . .?

GOULD: In your report on the book. It means something, it means a lot, I want to tell you, if you want to "do" something out here. A *freshness*, you said a *naïveté*, but call it a "freshness," and a capacity to get involved . . . I think that it's fantastic. And, you know, you dream about making a connection; but I feel I've *done* it.

KAREN: You've made a connection . . .

GOULD: Yes. And you reached out to *me*.

KAREN: I did . . .

GOULD: You shared this thing with me.

KAREN: . . . the book . . .

GOULD: You did it. Someone does something . . . *totally* . . .

KAREN: . . . yes . . .

GOULD: And you say "yes" . . . *"That's . . . that's* what I've been missing."

KAREN: . . . you're saying . . .

GOULD: That's what I've been missing. I'm saying, you come *alive,* and you see everyone's been holding their *breath* in this town, twenty years, forever, *I* don't know . . . and then . . .

KAREN: Yes . . .

GOULD: So rare, someone shows, shows some *enthusiasm* . . . it becomes, it becomes *simple.* You know what I mean . . .

KAREN: Yes. I do.

GOULD: N'I want to thank you. *(Pause.)*

KAREN: Um . . . it's nothing.

GOULD *(simultaneously with "nothing")*: It's something. No. Let, let, let, let me *help* you. That's what I want to do.

KAREN *(pause)*: I'm confused.

GOULD: I'm saying I *thank* you; I want to do something for you.

KAREN: No, no . . .

GOULD: And, whatever, I'm saying, if I can, that you would like to do, in, in the *Studio,* if you would like to do it, if I can help you with it, then I would like to help you.

KAREN: Yes. *Thank* you. *(Pause.)* I absolutely do. You *know* what I want to do.

GOULD: I . . .?

KAREN: I want to work on the film.

GOULD: Alright. If we can. The *Prison* film . . .

KAREN: No. On this. *This* film. The Radiation film and I don't care. I don't care in what capacity, well, why *should* I, 'cause I don't have any skills . . . *that's* presumptious, of *course*, in any way I could. But I'd just like, it would be so important to me, to *be* there. To help. (*Pause.*) If you could just help me with that. And, seriously, I'll get coffee, I don't care, but if you could do that for me, I would be . . . (*Pause.*)

GOULD: Hmmm.

KAREN: I've put you on the spot.

GOULD: No. Yes, a little.

KAREN: I'm serious. I'd do *anything* . . .

GOULD (*pause*): Look . . . (*Pause.*) This was a "courtesy read."

KAREN: I know that, but . . .

GOULD: As I told you, the chances were, were astronomically slim that it would . . .

KAREN: Of course, but you said, you, you wanted to *investigate* . . .

GOULD: . . . yes . . .

KAREN: . . . "because once in a while" . . .

GOULD: . . . yes.

KAREN: And once in a while one finds a pearl . . .

GOULD: Yes . . .

KAREN: And *this* book . . . I'm *telling* you, when you *read* it . . .

GOULD: Karen, it's about the End of the World.

KAREN: That's what I'm *saying*. That's why it . . .

GOULD: It's about the End of the World.

KAREN: Uh huh, uh huh. (*Pause.*) This book . . . (*Pause.*) This book . . . (*Pause.*) But you said someone's job was to read the manuscripts. (*Pause.*)

GOULD: Someone reads the manuscripts. Yes.

KAREN: . . . that come in . . .

GOULD: . . . yes. (*Pause.*) We have readers.

KAREN: Now: why do the readers read them?

GOULD (*simultaneously with "read"*): I get it. I get it. Yes. As I said. Yes. Once in a while, in a great while, yes, that . . .

KAREN: Why not this? I'm telling you . . .

GOULD: Look: I'm going to pay you the compliment of being frank. (*Pause.*) I'm going to talk to you. (*Pause.*) *Power*, people who are given a slight power, tend to think, they think that they're the only one that has these ideas, pure ideas, whatever, no matter. And, listen to me. Listen. I'm going to tell you. This book. Your book. On The End of the World which has meant so much to you, as I see that it has: Won't Make A Good Movie. Okay? I could tell you many things to influence you. But why? I have to respect your enthusiasm. And I *do* respect it. But this book, you want us to make, won't Get The Asses In The Seats. Sounds crass? Whatever the thing just may be. My job: my job, my new job ... is not even to "make," it is to "suggest," to "push," to champion ... good work, I hope ... choosing *from* Those Things Which the Public Will Come In To See. If they don't come to see it, what's the point? You understand? (*Pause.*) This is what I do. You said a certain kind of courage to embrace a fact? (*Pause.*) This is the fact here.

KAREN: Why do you ... (*Pause.*) Your job is to make movies people will come see.

GOULD: That's right.

KAREN: Why do you think they won't come see this one? (*Pause.*) Are you ever wrong? Do you see what I'm asking? Just because you think it is "too good" ... I ... I ... I think they would come see it. (*Pause.*) I would. It's about ... it's about what we feel. (*Pause.*)

GOULD: It is?

KAREN: Yes.

GOULD: Which is ...

KAREN: Everyone is frightened.

GOULD: Everyone is frightened.

KAREN: Everything is breaking down.

GOULD: It is?

KAREN: Yes.

GOULD: It is?

KAREN: Yes. It's over ...

GOULD: It ...

KAREN: I believe it is.

GOULD: . . . the . . .

KAREN: . . . things as we know them.

GOULD: Are over?

KAREN: Of course they are. Do you see? We don't have to *deny* it . . . The *power* that this thought will release . . . in, in, in *everyone*. Something which speaks to them . . . this book spoke to *me*. It *changed* me . . . I . . .

GOULD: Yes, but quite frankly the fact that it changed *you*, that *you* like it, that you'd like to see it "go" is not sufficient reason for the studio to pay fifteen million dollars to put it up there.

KAREN: A sufficient reason.

GOULD: Yes.

KAREN: To make the film.

GOULD: Yes. *(Pause.)*

KAREN: Someone, someone makes a decision to, someone can make a decision to . . .

GOULD: Richard Ross.

KAREN: You're going to see him tomorrow, you could . . . look. Look, I *read* the script. Mister Fox's script, the prison film. That's, that's just *degradation*, that's the same old . . . it's despicable, it's . . . It's degrading to the human spirit . . . it . . .

GOULD: It *what* . . . ?

KAREN: Of course; this rage . . . it's killing people, meaningless . . . the sex, the titillation, violence . . . people don't want, they don't *want*, they . . . they don't want this.

GOULD: Of course they do, that's what we're in business *to* do, don't you underst . . . that's what we're in business to do. *Make the thing everyone made last year. Make that image people want to see.* That *is* what they, it's more than what they want. It is what they require. And it's my job. That's my job . . . when I tell Ross about the Douglas Brown film, he's going to fall upon my neck and *kiss* me. *You* know that. *You* know that I can't make this book.

KAREN: I *don't* know that.

GOULD: I *told* you . . .

KAREN: You held out a hope to me, this morning . . .

GOULD: . . . I held out a hope . . .

KAREN: . . . that what I said . . .

GOULD: Aha! You see? That what *you* said . . . We all, as I said, everyone has feelings, *everyone* would like to "make a difference." Everyone says "I'm a maverick" but we're, *you* know that, just one part of the whole, nobody's a maverick.

KAREN: But . . .

GOULD: Now: what I told you was: it was a "courtesy read."

KAREN: . . . I, I don't like to be naïve . . .

GOULD: . . . I told you what the chances were . . .

KAREN: . . . I don't think it's attractive, and I don't think it's right. To be naïve. But . . .

GOULD: I *told* you what the deal was. Don't you understand?

KAREN: But I . . .

GOULD: But *you*. Yes. Everyone Is Trying To "Promote" Me
. . . Don't you *know* that? Don't you *care*? Don't you
care? Every move I make, do you understand? Everyone *wants* something from me.

KAREN (*pause*): Yes. I understand that.

GOULD: You understand that?

KAREN: Yes, I do.

GOULD: Well, if you understand that, then *how can you
act this way*?

KAREN: To come here . . .

GOULD: Yes.

KAREN: . . . you asked me here. (*Pause.*) I knew what the
deal was. I know you wanted to sleep with me. You're
right, I came anyway; you're right.

GOULD: . . . to sleep with you . . .

KAREN: Didn't you?

GOULD: No . . .

KAREN: Why lie? You don't have to lie.

GOULD: But you're wrong.

KAREN: But I'm *not* wrong. This is what I'm saying. Are
we so *poor* . . . that we can't have those simple things:
we want love, why should we deny it. Why should
you? You could of asked me, you *did* ask me. I know
what you meant. That's why I came.

GOULD: You came to . . .?

KAREN: I said why not? I'm weak, too. We all need companionship, the things we want ... I wanted them. You're right. I shouldn't act as though I was naïve. I shouldn't act as though I believed you. You're ... but but but:

GOULD: I asked you here to sleep with me?

KAREN: Then I read the book. I, I, I've been depraved, too, I've been frightened, I know that you're frightened. I *know* what you are. You see. That's what I'm telling you.

GOULD: *I'm* frightened ...

KAREN: I know that you are. I would have come here anyway. Is that depraved? *I* know what it is to be bad. I've been bad, I know what it is to be lost, I know you're lost. *I know* that ... How we are afraid ... to "*ask*," to even "ask," and say in jest, "Yes. I prayed to be pure" ... but it was not an accident. That I came here. Sometimes it reaches for us. And we say "show me a sign." And when it reaches us, then we see we *are* the sign. And we find the answers. In the book ...

GOULD: Why did you say you would come here anyway ...

KAREN: ... listen to me: The Tramp said "Radiation." Well, *whatever* it had been, it makes no difference ... Listen (*she reads*): "What was coming was a return to the self, which is to say, a return to God. It was round. He saw all things were round. And the man saw that it all had been devoted to one end. That the diseases in the body were the same diseases in the world. That things were ending. *Yes*. That things *must* end. And that vouchsafed to him a vision of infinity ..." You see?

GOULD: No.

KAREN: No?

GOULD: No, I don't understand.

KAREN: You don't understand.

GOULD: No.

KAREN: Would you like to understand? (*Pause.*) The things you've hoped for. The reason you asked me here.

GOULD: I don't understand you.

KAREN: You wanted something—you were frightened.

GOULD: I was frightened?

KAREN: That forced you to lie. I forgive you.

GOULD: ... you forgive me ...?

KAREN: You know how I can? Because we're just the same. You said you prayed to be pure.

GOULD: I said that ...

KAREN: This morning.

GOULD: I was joking.

KAREN: I looked in your heart. I saw you. And people can need each other. That's what the book says. You understand? We needn't be afraid.

GOULD: I don't understand.

KAREN: You can if you wish to. In the world. Dying. We prayed for a sign. A temporary girl. You asked read the book. I read the book. Do you know what it says? It says that you were put here to make stories people need to see. To make them less afraid. It says in *spite*

of our transgressions—that we could do something.
Which would bring us alive. So that we needn't feel
ashamed. (*Pause.*) We needn't feel frightened. The
wild animal dies with pride. He didn't make the
world. God made the world. You say that you prayed
to be pure. What if your prayers were answered? You
asked me to come. Here I am.

THREE

Gould's office. The next morning. GOULD *is sitting behind his desk.* FOX *enters.*

FOX: Okay. The one, the one, the one thing, I was up all night; I'm sorry, I should be better at these things, I don't know how to say it, you know how you do? You stand and think, you think, and, the only thing, one hand you say: "Am I worthy to be rich?" The other hand, you, you know, you feel *greedy*; so it's hard to know what's rightfully yours . . . Bob: when we said, when we said: *yesterday*: we were talking, when you said "producer"; what we *meant*, what we were talking about was, I understand it, that we were to "share" above-the-title, we would co-produce, because . . . that's right, isn't it? And the other thing; I'm sure you thought of this; to *say* to Ross, to, that we, as a team, you and I, this is only the *beginning*, for, if we brought *this* (I'm sure you thought of this) it's fairly limitless, we can bring *more* . . . those two things, only, what I wanted to say to you . . .

GOULD: I'm not going to do the film.

61

FOX: Which film?

GOULD: The Douglas Brown film.

FOX: . . . you're not . . .

GOULD: I'm not going to greenlight the Doug Brown prison film.

FOX: I don't blame you. It's a piece of shit. I were you, I'd do the film on Radiation. That's the project I would do. "A Story of Love, a Story of Hope." That's what I would do; and then spend the rest of my life in a packing crate. I can't get over those guys. Why do they waste our time? A talky piece of puke. Prestige and all, *okay*, but why, we should just say, "Sir, Sir, *you* go to the movies . . . if *you* saw a movie of this shit, would you sit through it?" Eastern Office sent the coverage to me—listen to this . . . (*He hunts through his papers. Reads.*) "The Bridge; or, Radiation, Half-Life and Decay of Society," the Blah Blah . . . set in novel form, The Growth of Radiation, as . . . "What is this? the device of *God*, in all things, to prepare the world for its final decay." Yeah. It's a *Summer* picture. (*Pause. Reads again.*) "The author seems to think that radio and television, aircraft travel and microwaves were invented solely to irradiate the world and so bring about genetic change in humankind." Great. And Scene Two, he comes out of the bar to find that his horse is gone and he has to go steal the sheriff's nag to ride for help. I'm sorry. I need a drink. Ten o'clock in the morning and I need a drink. You know, you look forward to something and you think it's never going to happen—and you *really* think, bullshit aside, it's never going to happen, and I've got to say, it's *over*, now, yeah, *yeah*, I felt a certain amount of *jealousy*, toward you, here we started out together, and I always said, someday I'll, you know, I'll get something for myself, and it'll be a Brand New Ballgame. I'll sit up there *with* Bobby Gould ... *over* him ... you know how we think. Deep inside, I never thought I would. (*Pause.*) And the *other* thing, talk about envy, is, a certain extent, I was riding, several years, on your *coattails* ... don't say "no," I know I was, and I want to thank you, that you were *man* enough, that you were *friend* enough, you never brought it *up*, you never rubbed it in. And I'm *glad* I can pay it back. Speaking of paying it back. Do I owe you, for sure, the five c? Fess up. (*Pause.*)

GOULD: Five c?

FOX: The broad come to your house?

GOULD: The broad?

FOX: You fuck the temporary girl? You fuck her. (*Pause.*)

GOULD: I'm going to go see Ross myself.

FOX: You're going to see him yourself. (*Pause.*) Without me, you're saying. (*Pause.*) Do you think that ... (*Pause.*) Do you think that that's the ... I mean ... it was ... if you think that that's the thing, then that's it. If you think that that's the thing, but, we should, we should, I think we should *talk* about it Bob. Don't you ... (*Pause.*) It was, um, um, uh (*Pause.*) I brought you the picture, Bob.

GOULD: I know you did.

FOX: You see what ... (*Pause.*) I, I, *I* think that we should go in there together. (*Pause.*) Babe. If this is truly a collaborative thing. (*Pause.*) But if you think that ...

GOULD: I'm not going to take him the Prison Film.

FOX: . . . if you think that that's the . . .

GOULD: . . . are you listening to me? I'm not going to greenlight the pris . . .

FOX: . . . sure, sure, sure . . . I understand that, but listen to what I'm asking you. Since I "brought" . . . which, I was saying, since, since I *brought* you the film and since, you say, we're going to split the credit. Because, because what I was *saying*, Bob, to to, finally get a position where I can be *equal*; where *I* brought *you* the film, it means a lot to me, and, frankly, um, um, I think . . .

GOULD: I'm not going to recommend the prison picture.

FOX: Okay. (*Pause.*) Is there . . . you're not . . .

GOULD: No. (*Pause.*)

FOX: I don't understand.

GOULD: I'm not going to recommend the Doug Brown film. (*Pause.*)

FOX: Because . . . hold on a second . . . hold on a second, before we get to that. You told me yesterday that we were going to go to Ross to greenlight it.

GOULD: Yes.

FOX: You promised me.

GOULD: I know.

FOX: I know that you know. Do you know *why* . . . ? Because you *did* it.

GOULD: I know that I did.

FOX: You're joking, right?

GOULD: No. (*Pause.*)

FOX: Huh. (*Pause.*) Because, um, you know, I had the package, Doug gave me one day, Doug Brown gave me the one day to have the package, I could have, I could have *took* the thing across the street, you know that? Walked right across the street, As People Do In This Town, and I'd done it *yesterday*, I'd been Executive Producer of a Doug *Brown* film. *Yesterday. Yesterday.* Which is what comes up when you tell me that you aren't going to . . . This is a joke. Right? I'm sorry . . . *I'm* sorry. Bob: When you take the film to Ross . . .

GOULD: I'm not going to take the film to Ross.

FOX (*pause*): Can you tell me why you're not?

GOULD: I'm going to greenlight the book.

FOX: What book?

GOULD: The Radiation book.

FOX: No, you aren't.

GOULD: Yes. If I can I am.

FOX: I have to siddown. (*Pause.*) Hold on a second, Bob, you're seeing Ross when . . .?

GOULD: Twenty minutes.

FOX: I'm not upset with you. (*Pause.*) Alright. (*Pause.*) Bob (*pause*): Now, listen to me: when you walk in his door, Bob, what you're paid to do . . . now, listen to me now: is make films that make money—you are paid to *make films people like.* And so gain for yourself a *fortune* every day. This is what Ross *pays* us for. This is the thing he and the stockholders want from us. This is what the, listen to me now, 'cause I'm going to "say" it, Movie Going Public wants from us, excuse me, I'm talking to you like some Eastern Fruit, but *this*, what I've just told you, is your job. You *cannot* make the radiation book.

GOULD: I'm going to try.

FOX: Shut up, I'm not done speaking, when it's your turn you can speak—because Ross will not do it and he will not *let* you do it.

GOULD: I have it in my contract. I can greenlight one picture a year under ten mil, at my discretion, without his prior approval or consent.

FOX: You will find your contract's shit.

GOULD: I don't think so.

FOX: Think so or not, you will find it's a *sucker* clause. You will find that if you insist on it you're going to become a laughingstock, and no one will *hire* you. Bob . . . You'll be "off the Sports List." *Why*? Because they will not understand why you did what you did. You follow me . . .? That is the *worst* pariah. Your best *friend* won't hire you. *I* won't hire you. Because I won't understand why you did the thing that you did, and tried to make a movie that no one will watch. Are you *insane*? What the fuck's *wrong* with you . . .? Have you read this book?

GOULD: Have you?

FOX: I read the coverage. What do you want from me? Blood? List . . . list . . . listen to this . . . (FOX *hunts on the desk for the book, opens it, reads*:) " ' . . . the world is dying,' he said, 'there is nothing we can do for that,' as he stood on the bridge. 'It all proliferates. Faster and

faster. It begets itself, until it's time to die. The econ-
omy will collapse. The reactors *will* explode, because
that's what they're meant to do. We will die, because
that's what *we're* meant to do. The radiation, which
has grown over the years, faster and faster.' " (*He puts
the book down.*)

GOULD: We have different ideas, Charlie.

FOX: We do? Since when . . .?

GOULD (*simultaneously with "when"*): I was up all night
thinking.

FOX: Were you?

GOULD: Yes.

FOX: Thinking about what?

GOULD: The . . .

FOX: Yes? (*Pause.*)

GOULD: The . . . why I was called to my new job.

FOX: Why you, uh huh . . .

GOULD: The notion, yes the notion that our life is *short* . . .
The . . . that, in some way . . .

FOX: Go on.

GOULD: I . . . I believe in the ideas that are contained in the
book.

FOX: Hey, I believe in the Yellow Pages, Bob, but I don't
want to *film* it. Bobby. Bobby. Why are you doing this?
Why are you doing this to me?

GOULD: You, *you* can take the prison film to Ross.

Fox: I take Ross the film, he'll make the film, and he'll give me a "thank you." You know that. I need *you*. I need your *protection* . . .

Gould: I . . .

Fox: You're going toidy over my whole life.

Gould: I . . .

Fox: Have, Bob, have you always hated me?

Gould: No.

Fox: Some secret . . .

Gould: No.

Fox: Doubted my loyalty, my . . .

Gould: No.

Fox: Then, then why are you doing this?

Gould: I think . . .

Fox: I'm listening to you.

Gould: . . . that we have few chances . . .

Fox: I'm listening to you.

Gould: To do something which is right.

Fox: To do something which is right? To do someth . . .?

Gould: I want to read you something. (*Hunts in book. Reads:*) " 'Is it true,' she asked, 'that we are always in the same state of growth, the same state of decay as the world in which we live? If it is true is it not true that the world is then a dream, and delusion?' All this being true, then what remained to him was this: Nothing." (*Pause.*) "Nothing but God." (*Pause.*) I've wasted my life, Charlie. My life is a sham, it's true. But I think I found something.

FOX: Bob, what's happened to you . . .?

GOULD: . . . And I think your prison movie has a place . . . and I respect your . . .

FOX: I don't want your respect. Your respect *stinks*: You know why? You've proved yourself insane. You're gonna buy a piece of shit . . . you're gonna spend ten million dollars for a piece of *pussy*, you were "up all night . . ." You were up all night boffing the *broad*. Are you getting *old*? What is this? *Menopause*? Your "life is a sham"? Two days in the new job, you can't stand the strain . . .? They're going to invalid you out, your name will be a *punchline* in this town . . .

GOULD: . . . if the film doesn't work out here . . .

FOX: If the film . . .

GOULD: The radiation film.

FOX: Did you miss your *wake* up call . . . ? If the film doesn't work out here, you know what you got? Little Lambsy Divey. No One Will Touch You, do you understand . . .? You're throwing your life away. (*Pause.*) Listen to me: Bob (*pause*): Bob (*pause*): I have to tell you something . . . It's the secretary. She, what did she do to you . . .?

GOULD: She did nothing to me.

FOX: What is she, a witch?

GOULD: She did nothing, we, we talked . . .

FOX: You talked and you decided to throw your career away . . .? And my, and my, and *my* chances with it . . .

GOULD: . . . I don't want . . .

FOX: *Bullshit* what you want. *Bullshit.* I Could Of Gone Across the Street.

GOULD: . . . I don't . . .

FOX: *Fuck* you . . . *Fuck* you . . . (*He hits* GOULD.) *Fuck* you. Get up. (*He hits him again.*) I'll fucken' kill you right here in this office. All this bullshit; you *wimp*, you *coward* . . . now you got the job, and now you're going to *run* all over everything, like something broke in the *shopping* bag, you *fool*—your fucken' sissy film— you squat to pee. You old *woman* . . . all of my life I've been eating your shit and taking your leavings . . . *Fuck* you, the Head of Production. Job I could of done ten *times* better'n you, the *press*, the *money*, all this time, and now you're going to be some fucken' *wimp*, cost me my, my, my . . . *fortune?* Not In This Life, Pal. Your Writ Has Run. You hear me . . .? (*Pause.*) Bob . . .? (*Pause.*) Do you hear me . . .? You want somebody to take charge? I'll take charge. Do you hear me, mis- ter . . .? You need an excuse to cop out, I'll give you your fucken' excuse. (*Pause.*) We have a meeting. Can you fix yourself up?

GOULD: No. (*Pause.*)

FOX: What's the matter?

GOULD: Nothing.

FOX: You have another shirt . . .? Can you get through the meeting with Ross?

GOULD: I'm going to greenlight the radiation book.

FOX: It's alright, Bob. It's okay. I see it now. It's okay. Everything is okay. Listen to me, it's alright. I'll explain it to you: a beautiful, a beautiful and an ambitious woman comes to ...

GOULD: I want you to be careful what you say about her.

FOX: It's only words, unless they're true. It's alright, now. I'm sorry I got frightened. Forgive me. I'll explain it to you. (*Pause.*) A beautiful and an ambitious woman comes to town. Why? Why does *anyone* come here ...? You follow my argument? (*Pause.*) Everyone wants power. How do we get it? Work. How do they get it? Sex. The End. She's different? Nobody's different. *You* aren't, *I'm* not, why should she? The broad wants power. How do I *know*? Look: She's out with Albert Schweitzer working in the jungle? No: she's here in movieland, Bob, and she trades the one thing that she's got, her *looks*, get into a position of authority—through you. Nobody likes to be promoted; it's ugly to see, but that's what happened, babe. I'm sorry. She lured *you* in. "Come up to my house, read this script ..." She doesn't know what that *means*? Bob: that's why she's here.

GOULD: ... A woman ...

FOX: ... Hey, pay me the courtesy ... how *lonely* you must be. How hard the world is. You complain to her. "No one understands me ..." "*I* understand you" ... she says.

GOULD: She *does* understand me.

FOX: Hey, that's *first-rate*.

GOULD: She *does* understand me ... she knows what I suffer.

FOX: "What You Suffer ..."? "What you suffer ..."? You're a *whore* ... Bob. You're a *chippy* ... you're a fucken' bought-and-paid-for *whore*, and you think you're a ballerina cause you work with your legs? You're a whore. You want some sympathy? You don't get none. You—you think you can let down. You *cannot* let down. That's what they pay the big bucks for. This is what you put up with you wanna have two homes. Okay? Bob, let's speak frankly, eh? This broad *just took you down.*

GOULD: . . . she came to me.

FOX: Why did she come to you? Cause you're the Baal Shem Tov? You stupid shit, I'm talking to you . . . Why does she come to you? 'Cause you're so good looking? She *wants* something from you. You're nothing to her but what you can *do* for her.

GOULD: You're full of shit.

FOX: Uh huh. I know I am.

GOULD: What does she want from me?

FOX: If I'm so smart? She wants you to greenlight this radiation book.

GOULD: Why?

FOX: The fuck should *I* know. *I* don't know. It's not important. Is she Head of Production? *You're* Head of Production. Read the new plaque on your door. Can she greenlight a film? No. *You* can. Now: what does she want from you? Hearth and Home? No. What? Love? Huh? Children? . . . To greenlight a film. To greenlight some bizarre idea . . .

GOULD: It's not a bizarre idea.

FOX: It's not a bizarre idea . . .? *Tell* it to me . . . Come on. You can't tell it to me in one sentence, they can't put it in T.V. Guide. What is this movie that you're going to make? Come on, "A Boy Joins the Cattle Drive and Learns to Be a Man ..."? "A Couple Finds a Million Dollars Buried in Their Yard ..."? Come on, come on ... what is this movie ...? (*Pause.*)

GOULD: We are ...

FOX: Tell me the story.

GOULD: We ... I'm *telling* it to you, and I don't think that we have to mock the possibility that someone could find something that meant something to them. You understand me?

FOX: Tell me the film, Bob.

GOULD: We ... I'll *tell* you the film. Alright? We are frightened ... (*Pause.*) Because the World is Ending. Uh ... (*Pause.*) A man gives up everything ... wait. (*Pause.*) A man, to find happiness ... (*Pause.*)

FOX (*picks up the book, reads*): "A gross infection rampant in the world, they spied, and thought they were the messengers of cure, when they were the disease" ... (*Turns page and reads again:*) "That silver is more powerful than gold; and the circle than the square or the triangle. He thought of architecture ..." (*He throws the book down.*) Are you kidding me ...? (*Pause.*) Are you kidding me ...? I wouldn't believe this shit if it was *true* ... the fuck *happened* to you? Let your dick run your *office*? What kind of a man ...

GOULD: Okay, Okay. That's enough.

FOX: I beg your pardon.

GOULD: I said that's enough Get out.

FOX: Fuck you.

GOULD: Fuck me. Fuck me in *hell*. Fuck me in hell, pal. *You* read the plaque on my door. I am you superior. Now, I've made my decision. I'm sorry it hurt you.

FOX: It hurt me? You ruined my life.

GOULD: Be that as it may.

FOX: I see.

GOULD: Now, I have a meeting.

FOX: Would you tell me why?

GOULD: I told you why. Because I've found something that's right.

FOX: I can't buy that.

GOULD: Then "why" is because I say so.

FOX: And eleven years down the drain.

GOULD: I'm sorry. (*Pause.*)

FOX: How sorry are you?

GOULD: What?

FOX: One question . . .

GOULD: It won't change my mind.

FOX: Well then, just say it's a boon, and grant it to me to assuage your guilt. I want to ask your girl one question. Then I swear I'll go.

GOULD: Alright—ask it.

FOX (*pushes the intercom button; into intercom*): Dear, could you come in here for one moment, please . . . ?

(KAREN enters.)

KAREN (to GOULD): What *happened* to you?

FOX: Where's *Cathy* ...?

KAREN: What happened to you, Bob ... are you alr ...

FOX: Where's Cathy, honey? She still sick ...?

GOULD: It's alright, Karen.

FOX: I have one question for you, and then I'll leave you alone. I understand ...

KAREN: I have to ... (*Starts to exit.*)

FOX: No, no, no, no, no ... No, no. It's alright. You alright, Bob?

GOULD: Yes.

FOX: Are you, really, though, *tell* us, now ...

GOULD: I'm fine. We'll be done here in one minute.

KAREN: What's going on?

GOULD: Just answer him.

FOX: I understand. Karen. I *understand* ... that things have been *occurring* ... large decisions ... do you follow me ...? (*Pause.*) Do you follow what I'm going to say?

KAREN: What do you want?

FOX: Well, Dear, I want to ask you something. (*Pause.*)

KAREN: Alright.

FOX: You went to Mister Gould's last night? (*Pause.*)

KAREN: Yes.

FOX: You discussed certain things?

KAREN: Yes. We did.

FOX: You talked about . . . his new job, you . . .

KAREN: You know what we talked about. We *talked* about
. . . we talked about not being frightened. We talked
about the ability to make a difference.

FOX: To make a difference. Yes.

KAREN: To make a film . . .

FOX: To make a film that makes a difference. Yes, I know.
Now: listen: I'm not going to talk to you of what gives
you the "insight" to, or the experience to know what
will make a good film. (*Pause.*) I'm not going to ask
you, I'm not going to ask you what, what brought you
to this job . . .

KAREN: . . . it was a temporary job . . .

FOX: Uh huh . . . I'm almost there, bear with me. Now: I
understand, last night, that you and Bob became inti-
mate.

KAREN: I think you should leave.

FOX: I know you do, but this is something more than your
life, honey, you're at the Big Table, and, I'm done, then
Bob, the Head of Production, is going to say what's
what. I have one question. Now, then, you and Bob,
you became "Lovers."

GOULD: Leave her alone.

FOX: I don't think so. Do you owe me this? Do you *owe* me
this? For all the years I spent with you? You became
lovers. (*Pause.*)

KAREN: Bob? No? Alright. Then, yes. We did.

FOX: You talked of love.

KAREN: Is that . . .

FOX: Did . . .?

KAREN: Is that so impossible . . .?

FOX: It's not impossible. No. Not at all. You were drawn to him. You were drawn to a man. It's not impossible, I think that we would say it happens all the time; you "said" things to each other. (*Pause.*) Things occurred. And this is serious. Forgive me if my words seem to belie that, but I'm doing all I can, 'cause I love this guy, too. My *question*: you answer me frankly, as I know you will: you came to his house with the pre-conception, you wanted him to greenlight the book. (*Pause.*)

KAREN: Yes.

FOX: If he had said "No," would you have gone to bed with him?

KAREN (*pause*): I don't think that I'll answer you.

FOX: No?

KAREN: I don't think you have the right to ask it. Bob . . .

GOULD: *I* would like to know the answer.

KAREN: You would.

GOULD: Yes. I would. (*Pause.*)

KAREN: Bob. Bob: the man I could respect . . .

GOULD: Without the bullshit. Just tell me. You're living in a World of Truth. Would you of gone to bed with me, I didn't do your book. (*Pause.*)

KAREN: No. (*Pause.*) No.

GOULD: Oh, God, now I'm lost.

FOX: Bob . . .

GOULD: Please be quiet for one moment.

KAREN: Bob. Bob, we have the opportunity . . .

FOX: "We"? "We" . . . ? I know who *he* is, who are *you*? Some broad from the Temporary Pool. A Tight Pussy wrapped around Ambition. That's who *you* are, Pal. Now you listen to me, Bob . . .

GOULD: Charlie. Please . . .

KAREN: We talked last night, Bob . . .

GOULD: You told me to Be a Man . . .

FOX: "Be a Man"? "Be a Man"? What right do you have? You know what this man has *done* . . . ? (*Phone rings,* FOX *picks it up. Into phone*:) Yes. One moment. Please . . . (*Hangs up.*)

GOULD: Oh, God. I don't know what to do.

FOX: You know the right thing to do.

KAREN: Bob, Bob. You reached out to me . . .

FOX: He reached out to you? He fucked you on a bet.

KAREN: I don't care.

FOX: You don't "care"?

KAREN: Bob, perfect love . . .

GOULD: Yes. Alright. Alright. Alright. Alright. Perfect Love. Alright. Just *stop* for a moment, will you? Will you? Will you just fucken' stop taking a *piece* of me for a moment. *Everyone.* Just *stop.* I need one moment, please.

KAREN: Bob, we decided last *night*.

GOULD: Yes. I'm *lost*, do you hear me, I'm *lost*. I have to think, I . . .

KAREN: We decided last night.

GOULD: We what?

KAREN: We decided last night.

FOX: Bob: I need you.

GOULD: I have to think.

FOX: I need you to remember me.

GOULD: I have to stop. I have to *think* now.

KAREN: Bob . . .

GOULD: . . . No.

KAREN: Bob, we have a meeting. (*Pause.*)

FOX: I rest my case. (*Pause.*)

KAREN: Did I say something wrong . . . ?

FOX: No. We have a meeting, that's true. Thank you, honey.

KAREN: Did I say something wrong . . . ?

FOX: Not at all. (*Picks up phone. Dials.*) Yes. Charlie Fox. Calling for Bob Gould. Mr. Gould and I have a . . . Yes. Mr. Ross is back from . . . ? Fine. Would you tell him we'll be just two, three minutes late? Thank you. (*Hangs up.*)

GOULD: I have to change my shirt.

KAREN: I don't understand.

GOULD: We're rather busy now. You'll excuse me. Mr. Fox will show you out.

KAREN: No. No. Listen to me. One moment. One moment, Bob. Wait, Bob. The things we said last night. You called for help. Bob, you remember? Listen to me. (*She picks up the book and starts to read*:) "One bell was 'showers about us': two bells was 'showers across the Lake'; three bells was 'showers across the Ocean'; and four bells was 'showers across the World.' And he wondered how they had obtained that concession to rehearse the bells for the benefit of this instruction." No, that's the wrong bit. That's not the part . . . (GOULD *exits to the washroom. She looks up.*) Bob . . . ?

FOX: That was a close one. Don't you think?

KAREN: I think I'm being punished for my wickedness.

FOX: Yeah, I do, too. You got a lot of nerve, Babe. And I'll tell you something else, that's why you're *stupid*, is you made your move on something wasn't *ever* going to make a movie. Cause the people wouldn't come. (*He picks up the book, reads*:) "The Earth burned. But the last man had a vision . . ."

KAREN: I don't belong here.

FOX: Well, I can help you out on that. You ever come on the lot again, I'm going to have you killed. Goodbye. See you at the A and P.

KAREN: Goodbye.

FOX: I heard you. (*Pause.*)

KAREN: What did I say . . . ?

FOX: . . . Uh huh . . .

KAREN: I don't understand.

FOX: I'll send you the coverage. (*Pause.*) Goodbye. You've said your piece. Now go away. (*Pause.*)

KAREN: I hope . . .

FOX: We *all* hope. It's what keeps us alive. (*Pause.* KAREN *exits. He picks up the book, throws it out after her.*) And take this with you. (*To himself:*) "How are things made round . . . (*GOULD reenters, tucking in his clean shirt. Pause.* GOULD *looks at* FOX.) Well, Bob, you're human. You think I don't know? I know. We wish people would like us, huh? To Share Our Burdens. But it's not to be.

GOULD: . . . I suppose not.

FOX: You're goddamn right, not. And what *if* this fucken' "grace" exists? It's not for you. You know that, Bob. You know that. You have a different thing.

GOULD: She told me I was a good man.

FOX: How would *she* know? You *are* a good man. Fuck *her*.

GOULD: I only wanted . . .

FOX: I know what you wanted, Bob.

GOULD: I only wanted . . .

FOX: I know what you wanted, Bob. You wanted to do good.

GOULD: Yes. (*Pause.*) Thank you.

FOX: Hey, what'd you want me to say, Bob, you "Owe" me . . .? (*Phone rings,* FOX *answers it. Into phone:*) We're coming . . . (*Hangs up.*) Because we joke about it, Bob, we joke about it, but it *is* a "People Business," what else is there . . . ?

GOULD: I wanted to do Good . . . But I became foolish.

Fox: Well, so we learn a lesson. But we aren't here to "pine," Bob, we aren't put here to *mope*. What are we here to do (*pause*) Bob? After everything is said and done. What are we put on earth to do?

Gould: We're here to make a movie.

Fox: Whose name goes above the title?

Gould: Fox and Gould.

Fox: Then how bad can life be?

Methuen Drama Contemporary Dramatists

include

John Arden (two volumes)
Arden & D'Arcy
Peter Barnes (three volumes)
Sebastian Barry
Dermot Bolger
Edward Bond (eight volumes)
Howard Brenton
  (two volumes)
Richard Cameron
Jim Cartwright
Caryl Churchill (two volumes)
Sarah Daniels (two volumes)
Nick Darke
David Edgar (three volumes)
David Eldridge
Ben Elton
Dario Fo (two volumes)
Michael Frayn (three volumes)
John Godber (three volumes)
Paul Godfrey
David Greig
John Guare
Lee Hall (two volumes)
Peter Handke
Jonathan Harvey
  (two volumes)
Declan Hughes
Terry Johnson (three volumes)
Sarah Kane
Barrie Keefe
Bernard-Marie Koltès
  (two volumes)
Franz Xaver Kroetz
David Lan
Bryony Lavery
Deborah Levy
Doug Lucie

David Mamet (four volumes)
Martin McDonagh
Duncan McLean
Anthony Minghella
  (two volumes)
Tom Murphy (five volumes)
Phyllis Nagy
Anthony Neilson
Philip Osment
Gary Owen
Louise Page
Stewart Parker (two volumes)
Joe Penhall
Stephen Poliakoff
  (three volumes)
David Rabe
Mark Ravenhill
Christina Reid
Philip Ridley
Willy Russell
Eric-Emmanuel Schmitt
Ntozake Shange
Sam Shepard (two volumes)
Wole Soyinka (two volumes)
Simon Stephens
Shelagh Stephenson
David Storey (three volumes)
Sue Townsend
Judy Upton
Michel Vinaver
  (two volumes)
Arnold Wesker (two volumes)
Michael Wilcox
Roy Williams (two volumes)
Snoo Wilson (two volumes)
David Wood (two volumes)
Victoria Wood

For a complete catalogue of Methuen Drama titles
write to:

Methuen Drama
36 Soho Square
London
W1D 3QY

or you can visit our website at:

www.methuendrama.com